Taking Care of Business:
What Family Members Need to Know

By

Lydia M. Douglas

PriorityBooks
PUBLICATIONS

P.O. Box 2535

Florissant, Mo 63033

Edited by: Lynel Johnson Washington

Cover Designed by Sheldon Mitchell of Majaluk

Manufactured in the United States of America

Library of Congress Control Number: 2007943852

ISBN 13: 978-09792823-8-6

ISBN 10: 0-9792823-8-1

All scriptures are taken from the King James Version of the Bible.

For information regarding discounts for bulk purchases, please contact Prioritybooks Publications at 1-314-741-6789 or rosbeav03@yahoo.com You can contact the author at ldoug48305@aol.com

Taking Care of Business:
What Family Members Need to Know

By

Lydia M. Douglas

PriorityBooks Publications

Florissant, Missouri

Table of Contents

Dedication

I dedicate the words of this book to my late husband, James H. Douglas, Sr., and to my three sons Gerry, Mark, and James Jr. James and I were married for 39 years. His death inspired me to write this book to share valuable information to help others. To all my church family at Shalom Church, City of Peace, who encouraged me to share my passions over the past two years by reading my columns and purchasing my first book, *Stepping Stones to Success,* I thank you for inviting me to speak and to share information through presentations and conversations. To Dr. F. James Clark, Pastor and Founder of Shalom Church, City of Peace, I thank you for your leadership. To each of you, I dedicate this book.

Thank you very much,

Lydia M. Douglas

The Douglas Family

Taking Care of Business:
What Family Members Need to Know

Introduction

When God created this earth and formed man in His image, one of His greatest commandments was that we love one another. One of the main precepts of love is sharing. Though sharing may seem like a foreign concept to many individuals, it is an essential act that unites souls. A prime example of the importance of sharing occurs when knowledge is passed on from one generation to the next. "Knowledge is power" is a famous mantra that is often expressed to emphasize the great need for continual learning. Since I sternly believe in the power of knowledge, I am taking this moment to pass on an essential bit of knowledge I have gained from my own personal experiences to you, my readers.

It is my desire that this book touches the heart and soul of its readers. I hope it inspires readers to consider getting their whole lives in order. We spend a lifetime working on our outer appearances, by trying to look our very best to not only impress ourselves but to impress others, as well. Yet, when it comes down to truly taking care of important business matters pertinent to our lives, we falter.

For the sake of this book, the important business matter I am referring to is the accumulation, preparation and documentation of all pertinent information warranted in case a severe illness strikes you and you need to be admitted to a nursing home or hospitalized for an extended period of time, or if your untimely death occurs. This paperwork includes insurance policies, computer passwords, the location of keys to security boxes, your last will and testament, and your pre-paid funeral and burial plan.

Disorder breeds contention, stress and frustration amongst siblings and other family members. Therefore, taking care of this essential business matter now is a necessity, which will lead to a greater sense of peace for you and a stronger sense of control for your family. Indeed, placing things in proper order frees one's mind from confusion and clutter. Ideally, your family will know and understand exactly how to handle your personal business affairs based upon your well-prepared information and your foresight will be appreciated.

In addition to teaching you the formalities of organizing your personal business matters, I have included some meaningful meditations and other tidbits to encourage your heart and soul.

Information Family Members Should Know

Information Family Members Should Know

God said in His word, "Do things decently and in order." Preparation is the key to order. By taking time now to adhere to the information listed below you can rest more peacefully knowing that your family members will be better organized, well-informed and know exactly what to do at the time of your unfortunate passing. The items are not listed in any particular order, but they all are very important steps to follow.

Get a fire proof filing cabinet, if you don't have one.

Purchase some file folders.

Record family members' dates of birth, social security numbers, bank account numbers, and employers' phone numbers in a file folder labeled "Important Dates and Contact Numbers."

Make it a point to share other private numbers/passwords with your family members, as well as pin numbers, your computer password, garage door code number, and house security system code.

Insert 401K, CD and IRA paperwork into a file labeled "Financial Portfolio."

Store all insurance policies, including homeowners, rental, auto, fire, flood, and/or hazard, as well as insurance policies/medical benefits/pension plans that you have obtained via your place of employment into a file labeled "Insurance." Include the name, address and phone number of the Human Resources Director at your job with your employment insurance paperwork.

If you still have a mortgage, document who it is financed through and log it in a file folder labeled "Mortgage."

If you have a car note, document where and whom it is financed through and label the file folder "Car Note."

Put your will in a file folder labeled "Will," if you have one; if not, get one drawn up immediately.

In addition to the regular will, get a Living Trust done. A Living Trust is much better to have than a regular will. It will protect your family from going to Probate Court. Going to Probate will cost a lot of money. If you cannot afford to do this you may want to invest in the Living Trust software that can be found in most stores. However, it is important to do things with the proper guidance to ensure that whatever you choose to do will be valid and non-revocable. If you don't want to be put on a respirator if an illness occurs, taking the route of a Living Trust is very important. This will give your family the right to relay your wishes to your doctor.

Make sure that your beneficiary information is up-to-date on everything.

Write down all medications and dosages that you are currently taking. Make three copies of this medication list; one for your medicine cabinet, one for your file cabinet, and one for the glove compartment of your car (This is very helpful if you have an accident or some other type of medical issue occurs while you are driving). Update it as needed. Also, record your doctor(s) name, address and phone number on your medication list.

Research where you would like to buried, then discuss this information with your family members.

All of this is vital information and will save time and heartache for your family members when the need for it arises. Tell your family where this important information is located. If they don't want to talk about it, tell them anyway. Even though this is one of the most important conversations families should have, it is one of the hardest. It is hard to discuss death because no one wants to imagine someone that they love not being around, Though not having this conversation can leave loved ones struggling to figure out what to do.

Be sure to go over all of the information with your loved ones, so that they will gain a clearer understanding of why these matters are so important to you.

Types of Wills

Types of Wills

It is important to take the proper steps to assure that your assets are distributed the way that you want them to be should something happen to you. Most people do not have wills. There are many reasons that this happens. Many people feel that there is no need, thinking that they do not have much to divide or to leave to their survivals. Others may feel that they cannot afford to pay for a will. Still others just put it off. It's hard to think that something may happen to you or to a loved one, so sometimes it is easier to just not talk about these kinds of issues. However, if you desire to avoid causing a rift between your relatives, developing a will is the best move you could possibly make.

There are two types of wills: Last Will and Testament and Living Trust Will.

Last Will and Testament

Anyone can use this will, including the elderly, young parents, or a single person with assets.

What is the purpose of the Last Will and Testament?

- To distribute your property and assets the way you want them to be distributed.
- To provide appropriately for your family
- To designate who you would like to receive your property
- To name a guardian for your minor children
- To create a trust for minor children

Living Trust Will

What happens if you are sick and cannot take care of yourself? Would you want to live in a nursing home? Or would you like to stay in your own home and have nurses attend to you in a place that you feel most comfortable? What if you could not speak or do for yourself? This is why having a Living Will is necessary. A Living Will ensures that your wishes are carried out and that your family members are free from having to make tough decisions about what should happen to you if extraordinary means are needed, such as in the case of artificial life support. This will protects your family from having to make such decisions while they are already grieving and in pain.

What is the purpose of a Living Will?

- It outlines what type of medical care you would like to receive in the event you become incapacitated.
- It states whether you would like to be resuscitated or incubated.
- It lets your family know if you want to be an organ donor.
- It specifies whether or not you want to receive artificial life support.

Power of Attorney

Another important factor to consider is who will make decisions for you should you become mentally and/or physically incompetent. This is when a Power of Attorney is useful. A Power of Attorney lets you appoint someone you trust to make legal decisions on your behalf. They are most often used in case of illness or incapacitation.

What will a Power of Attorney allow someone to do?

- Pay your bills
- Handle your financial transactions (banking, filing taxes, etc.)
- Allows the person chosen to buy, sell or manage your property and other real estate

Pre-Paid Funeral Plan

Pre-Paid Funeral Plan

I would like to share my experience with you regarding the importance of having a pre-paid funeral plan. I lost my husband on Sept. 30, 2007, and his service was held on October 5, 2007. Losing my husband was a very painful and hurtful feeling. Having his business and mine organized helped to ease any confusion that I could have experienced, because everything was in decent order.

God gave me the plan about eight years ago. I had to incorporate it into my budget. I made some sacrifices, and I did it. I did not know that I would be using it as soon as I did. I thought my kids would use it later down the road, for me or my husband.

I called a mortuary to find out as much as I could about pre-paid services, and then their representative came out to discuss a variety of plans with me. During the meeting the representative started off with the most expensive package, but I was in control and not my emotions. So I picked something that was more in line with my budget. I picked the plan I wanted. Mind you, I did not choose the most expensive one, nor did I choose the cheapest one. You see, my emotions were not at stake. These decisions are best made when you can think freely.

The plan included the casket, wake, limousine, church service and burial service. I only paid for one limousine. No need to pay for two or three for other family members, when they could drive their own cars.

You are required to make monthly payments on your plan until it is paid in full. Upon completion of your payments, they will send you a paid in full receipt along with your certificate and certificate number.

Now, this information is not held at the local mortuary, but it is in a trust in Jefferson City (the capital of Missouri) and it is transferable. So, if I leave the state of Missouri it is still good.

When my husband passed, I called the mortuary and brought my certificate to the office. A representative put the number in the system and everything came up Paid In Full. However, I did have to purchase the flowers I wanted and pay for the obituaries and extra death certificates. They give you one death certificate, but you must order extras, because when you close out a person's life, the insurance company and everyone else requests an original. You can't make copies from the original they give you.

The same thing holds true for the cemetery. The crypt, grave marker, as well as the opening and closing of the grave, were pre-paid. I had to purchase the crypt because of the water level where his site is located.

The best thing about planning early is the fact that you don't leave your family members with the burden of having to shop around to secure the best price to fit their current budget. I know a person who went to three different mortuaries looking for the best price, because his deceased family member did not have insurance or a bank account.

You might have life insurance, but insurance companies do not write the check immediately. So that means you have to use your savings in order to pay the bills until you get the check.

For those who are homeowners and/or car owners, please adhere to this crucial piece of advice: It is vital (I stress vital) that when you purchase your life insurance policy, make sure that there is enough coverage included to pay off the balance owed on your home and car, so that your surviving spouse/child(ren) or other loved one(s) can afford to render the balance owed, especially if you were the breadwinner.

I am thankful that I was obedient to what God gave me to do.

He knew; I didn't.

Thank you!!!

Important Forms and Other Information

The following forms are being provided to assist loved ones in taking care of business if the untimely death of a loved one happens to occur.

Please, as you complete the forms do not let the information frighten you. Answering the questions may prevent delays, answer lingering questions, and reduce worries.

The forms should only take about three hours to complete.

Personal Bequests

What to do with family heirlooms and sentimental items? Since most wills don't have personal items spelled out in detail, you can write the information down here.

Item	Name of person to receive it.	Where is the item located?

Funeral Instructions

It's scary to make your own funeral arrangements. Yet it is something you need to do. How else would anyone know what to do or where to bury you without this knowledge?

Name of family member

_____

_____

_____

Address

_____

_____

_____

Phone

_____

_____

_____

Date this was completed

_____

_____

Choice of Funeral Home

_____

_____

Type of preparation (check one)

☐ Regular burial   ☐ Cremation   ☐ Donate body

Type of funeral (check one)

☐ Memorial ☐ open casket ☐ closed casket ☐ other

If other was selected, please clarify

_____

_____

_____

_____

_____

Location of service

_____

_____

_____

_____

Location of cemetery

_____ ..

_____

Casket and vault preference

_____

_____

Pastor preference

_____

_____

Active Pall/Casket Bearer

_____ _____ _____

_____ _____ _____

_____   _____   _____

_____   _____   _____

Honorary Pall/Casket Bearer

_____   _____   _____

_____   _____   _____

_____   _____   _____

Music Preference

Soloists

_____| _____|_____

_____

Pianist

(1st choice)_____

(Alternate)_____

Organist

(1st choice)_____

(Alternate) _____

Songs_____

_____

_____

Favorite Scriptures _____

_____

_____

Pastor/Minister who will officiate _____

_____

_____

Type of flowers_____

_____

_____

Head Stone preference _____

_____

What you want in your obituary _____

_____

_____

_____

_____

_____

_____

_____

_____

_____

_____

_____

Other ideas or information_____

_____

_____

_____

_____

_____

Personal Thoughts

How do your parents feel about remarriage after the lost of their spouse? How do you feel?

_____

_____

_____

_____

_____

_____

_____

_____

What to do with your property? Should it be sold and money divided with survivors?

_____

_____

_____

_____

_____

_____

_____

What to do with the beloved animals?

_____

_____

_____

_____

_____

Other information

My Views on heroic measures taken for my medical care

This is just a sample. Please seek the opinion of an attorney about the laws of your state regarding a "living will" in your state.

I request that if there are reasonable expectations that I should recover from a mental or physical illness do all that is possible to preserve my life. However, if there is no reasonable expectation of my survival, I request that action should not be taken to keep me alive by artificial or heroic means. To avoid burdening my family in making decisions, it is my desire in the event of a grave illness and under the appropriate circumstances that this information is shared with the physician or physicians over my care. I request that my family adhere to my request as well as to the recommendations of my physician (s).

Signature of Wife: _____ Date _____

Signature of Spouse:_____ Date_____

Witnessed by:_____ Date_____

This is not a legal form. You should make arrangements to talk to your lawyer about how to best handle these issues. For medical information, talk to your doctor and he or she should lead you to the right people. If you want to be a donor you can complete a donor's card or sign the back of your driver's license.

Note: You can also complete a simple form for donating your body to a medical or research facility.

Where are my important papers?

Birth Certificates

Parents _____ Children _____
Adoption papers _____

Military discharge papers _____
Tax returns _____

Bank accounts _____

Citizenship papers _____

Insurances

Homeowners _____

Life _____

Health _____

Accident_____

Automobile_____

Business_____

Homeowners' deed _____

Cemetery plot _____

Copy of Wills _____

Burial Instructions _____

Divorce records _____

Trust agreements _____

Money Accounts

Banks

_____   _____   _____

Checking

_____   _____   _____

List of credit cards

_____   _____   _____

_____   _____   _____

Stock certificates

_____   _____   _____

_____   _____   _____

Other Important papers _____   _____

_____   _____

Important Numbers

Social Security Numbers

Name _____

Name _____

Name _____

Name _____

Name _____

Credit Card Numbers

Name _____

Name _____

Name _____

Name _____

Name _____

Checking Account Numbers

Name _____

Name _____

Name _____

Name _____

Name _____

Savings Account Numbers

Name _____

Name _____

Name _____

Safe Deposit Box Number

Location _____ Number _____

Safe Combination_____

Life Insurance

Insured's Name	Amount of Coverage	Policy Number	Agent or Company

Stock, Securities, or Mutual Funds

Owner	Present Value	Type of Asset	Certificate	Company of Agent to contact

List of Assets

Property	Description / Owner	Fair Market Value	Amount Owed	Original Cost
Other Real Estate				
Livestock				
Other				

Important Telephone Numbers

Doctors:

_____ _____ _____

Hospitals

_____ _____ _____

Lawyers

_____ _____ _____

Insurance Agents

_____ _____ _____

Banks

_____ _____ _____

To check on benefits, please call these organizations, who may pay partial burial benefits if the person served in the Armed Forces.

Veteran's Administration

_____ _____ _____

Social Security Administration

_____ _____ _____

Organizations the person belongs to

_____ _____ _____

Former and current employers

_____ _____ _____

Pension companies

_____ _____ _____

Health Insurance (may pay for the deceased last illness)

_____ _____ _____

IRA and Keogh Plans

_____ _____ _____

Names of Medications

_____ _____ _____

Other Telephone Numbers

_____ _____ _____

_____ _____ _____

_____ _____ _____

_____ _____ _____

Cremation

So many people have been negatively affected by the current economy, and have chosen to forego big funerals and burials for a memorial service and cremation.

Funeral providers will help find the best option for memorializing and cremation services.

After deciding on cremation you must think about a permanent placement of the cremated remains. To place the remains at your local cemetery is important for many reasons. First, a site close to your loved ones would make visitation easier. Second, you wouldn't want to leave the remains with loved ones because they could become mistakenly misplaced or discarded over the years. This is likely to happen if the holder of the urn passes away and their children do not feel the same way about the deceased.

Third, with a ceremony and the placement of the urn in a cremation garden in a cemetery the family members receive closure after the loss of their loved one. Finally, location is important for current and future generations to visit when researching their heritage.

Be sure to determine how you plan to pay for the cremation process beforehand.

If you decide to pay in advance, which is the best way in my opinion, do not make payment directly to the funeral home. A funeral home could go out of business. Prearrangement guarantees that your plan will pay for the funeral you prearranged regardless of how long you live or how much the funeral cost has increased since the time you made the prearrangement.

Additional Information
You May Need To Know

Personal Contacts

We need to have personal contact information handy and updated on a regular basis.

It is a necessity to keep up with the changing times and technology due to people regularly changing their phone numbers, email addresses and other pertinent information. Do any of us know anyone's phone number by heart anymore?

We need to make a list of family members, friends, neighbors, or other important contacts who can come help us quickly in our time of need.

Contact List for Emergencies

Name: _____

Relationship:_____

Telephone:_____

Name: _____

Relationship:_____

Telephone:_____

Name: _____

Relationship:_____

Telephone:_____

Name: _____

Relationship:_____

Telephone:_____

There are two reasons you need to list the phone number of people you know who can help you or your family make important decisions about you and your family. These people can be close relatives, your pastor or a responsible child you selected to oversee your interests. The people are the ones who will know what to do in case of emergency or in the event of your unfortunate death.

The people listed are the ones who know you and can provide information on about you in the event it is needed. These are the people you have shared your desires with about your obituary, funeral, services, what to do in event of an emergency and so much more.

Names and Phones Numbers

When I need to talk to someone:

Family

Names:_____

Phone Numbers:_____

Friends

Names:_____

Phone Numbers:_____

Pastor:

Names:_____

Phone Numbers:_____

Church:

Names:_____

Phone Numbers:_____

Neighbors:

Names:_____

Phone Numbers:_____

Occupation, job title, and the length of service that was performed.

Your Job or Employer:

Company and Phone Number:_____

_____

Doctor's name: _____

Phone number: _____

More Things to Add to Your Obituary

Have you written your obituary? Do your family and friends know what kind of work you did and who you worked for? Did you volunteer for an organization? Is there a charity close to your heart that you would want donations to be sent to in your memory? Since you know you better than anyone else, it would be great if you could write your own obituary. If you are uncomfortable doing this, make sure that the people who will be responsible for pulling all your information together have all the information you want to share with others.

In your obituary, please add some valuable information such as:

- Full name, names of parents, brothers and sisters, deceased and alive.

- Educational attainment. Did you graduate from high school or college? What is the name of the college and what city is it located in?

- City and state of birth. Where were you born? Does your family have this information?

- Who should be contacted in the event of your death? Make a list and add the phone numbers.

- Contacts that need to be made ASAP:

- Funeral Director

- Family, relatives and friends

- Cemetery information to be given to Funeral Director

- Newspaper if you want to be placed in the local paper

- Social Security Administration.

If you are frustrated, sad and overly burdened during this difficult time, stop, breathe in and exhale. Read and be comforted by II Corinthians 1:3-4 KJV

"Blessed be God, even the Father of our Lord Jesus Christ, the Father of mercies, and the God of all comfort. Who comforteth us in all our tribulations, that we may be able to comfort them which are in any trouble, by the comfort wherewith we ourselves are comforted of God."

Meditations

I have written these meditations to help inspire you and to assure you that when you read and study God's words, they will bring you truth and understanding. God's words reveal to us that he is indeed our protector and our strength through the good times and the bad times. These Bible verses helped me in my understanding of God's plan and how His will affected my life.

Standing On The Strength of God

Psalm 46:1, 10

"God is our refuge and strength, a very present help in trouble."

"Be still, and know that I am God, I will be exalted among the heathen, I will be exalted in the earth."

God is our refuge and our strength. He is there when we think He is not. That is when we can look back and see that we are truly standing on God's strength. We have trials and tribulations but our struggles come to make us strong. If we allow ourselves to be used by God, He will do just as He said He would do.

I am so grateful and thankful for all that God has done in my life. God said, "Be still, and know that I am God, I will be exalted among the nations, I will be exalted in the earth. The Lord God Almighty is with us, the God of Jacob is our fortress."

While we are being still, we should ask God to help us to be still in the right way, not angry or bitter or mean to others. God gave me specific instructions to be still, wait on the Him and put on the garment of praise in the midst of my heaviness so that He may be glorified.

We do have a part to play in receiving God's blessings. In the midst of my pain, I am still praising Him for the good and happy times He gave me with my husband. He was by far my husband and my best friend. Also, he was a good father to our three sons, Gerry, Mark, and James, Jr.

My trials have been stress free all because I was obedient to what God told me to do in 1999. Because I was obedient I am standing on His strength and have been able to endure all I have gone through.

It is very important that we do what God instructs us to do. After all, He knows our tomorrows, He knows our beginnings and our endings. We do indeed reap what we sow. We have a choice of being obedient or disobedient to God's voice.

Had I not been obedient to what God said, I would not have been able to reap the benefits of a stress free time in my life.

I can truly say I have been blessed.

Garment of Praise

Isaiah 61:3

Ephesians 6: 10-17 addresses "Putting on the whole armor of God…" He did not say take it off. We are to keep it on morning, noon and night.

Now, I read in Isaiah 61:3. "To appoint unto them that mourn in zion, to give unto them beauty for ashes, the oil of joy for mourning, the garment of praise for the spirit of heaviness: that they might be called the trees of righteousness, the planting of the Lord, that He might be glorified." And we are to keep that on as well.

When we are going through the heaviness of life, God promised to comfort all who mourn. God said He would exchange the evidence of mourning with the evidence of rejoicing. Our ashes would be exchanged for beauty.

God would give a garment of praise for the spirit of heaviness, in order for Him to be glorified. He promised to give a garment of praise, instead of a spirit of despair. As long as we stay connected to Him, He will give us that garment of praise. With the garment of praise on, we will be able to walk through the valley of the shadow of death and fear no evil, because then, we will know that He is with us.

In order that we do not encounter fear, we must put on the garment and keep it on. In the midst of my loss, God has given me that garment of praise. He said in His word that when we leave mother and father we are no longer twain but one.

When God reached down and called one of His servants home, that was actually one half of me, but He promised me that He would rebuild that half and He is doing just that. Actually, He is doing that and much more. More than I would have ever expected.

My strength is being renewed day by day. God said weeping may endure for a night, but joy cometh in the morning. When we keep our garment on, and we find ourselves in the midst of our heaviness, He will let us know that He is our keeper and the lifter up of our heads.

God is sovereign, and He can get us through any situation that we find ourselves in. We don't know what our tomorrows have in store for us, but we know who holds our tomorrows and on that He desires all of our praise.

I thank God for protecting me,

For watching over me,

For keeping me;

He deserves all of my praise.

I know that earth has no sorrow that Heaven cannot heal.My strength lies in the praise I give to God. So how are we dressed on today? Let's all put on, and keep on, the garment of praise, in order that we might glorify God, no matter what He allows us to go through.

He is still worthy of all of our praise!!!!!

Something to Think About

With all of the tragedies that are happening in this world, I look around and see people who have problems much greater than mine. Yet they confront life with a courageous and honest determination within themselves. It makes me stop and realize how small my worries are in comparison and how I should try that much harder to be happy, tolerant, understanding and caring toward others.

It encourages me to believe in my own abilities, but most of all to be thankful for all I have everyday of my life. I have learned that, at any given moment a smile can change one's direction, and who is to know when a smile is needed by someone else.

Nothing is worth more than this day, tomorrow is not promised to anyone.

Shalom--Peace

Comfort Comes in Trusting God

John 14: 13-18

"And whatsoever ye shall ask in my name, that will I do that the Father may be glorified in the Son. If ye ask anything in my name I will do it. If ye love me, keep my commandments. And I will pray the father, and He shall give you another Comforter, that He may abide with you forever. Even the Spirit of truth; whom the world cannot receive, because it seeth him not, neither knoweth him, but ye know him; for he dwelleth with you and shall be in you. I will not leave you comfortless: I will come to you."

When we feel like we are at the end of our rope, we need a reminder of who is really at the end of the ROPE. It is Jesus, Himself. And He is standing in the gap for us.

He will take all of our hurts, disappointments and needs, whatever we are going through, He will take them to the Father. He said the only way to the Father is by and through Him. By this, we can have comfort by trusting in the Lord, because we know all of our cares will be met.

2 Corinthians 4: 8-9 says:

"We are troubled on every side, yet not distressed; we are perplexed, but not in despair; persecuted, but not forsaken; cast down, but not destroyed."

But for which cause we faint not, although our outward man perish, yet the inward man is renewed day by day. He said our light afflictions, which are, for a moment, worketh for us, a far more exceeding and eternal weight of glory. He said our light afflictions are for a moment, but sometimes our affections do not seem light at all. He also said 1000 years is as a day with the Lord.

We cannot figure Him out, we just have to believe. When we have faith in our Lord and Savior Jesus Christ that is a treasure we have in these earthen vessels. We have to know that the excellency of the power is of God and not us. When He allows us to do something, we have to give Him the credit. We cannot do anything without God. He is the author and the finisher of our faith.

Whatever we want, if it is written in His Word, and it is His will for us, it will come to pass, because He is a God that cannot lie. If we put our trust in God all of our needs will be met. All we have to do is ask, and His will, will be done in our lives. His will is always best for us.

Sometimes, our days seem dark and dim. Sometimes, we cannot see our way. But Isaiah 40: 29-31, says: "He giveth power to the faint; and to them that have no might he increaseth strength. Even the youths shall faint and be weary, and the young men shall utterly fall: But they that wait upon the LORD shall renew their strength; they shall mount up with wings as eagles; they shall run, and not be weary; and they shall walk, and not faint."

There is comfort in trusting in the Lord. If we keep our trust in Christ Jesus and faint not, we will be comforted above measure. He did not bring any of us this far to leave us. He carried all of our cares and burdens to the cross with

Him. No matter what it is that we might face, He already knows about it. All we have to do is trust in Him. He also said in His word: He will never leave us, nor forsake us.

Proverbs 3: 1-6

"My son, forget not my law; but let thine heart keep my commandments: For length of days, and long life, and peace, shall they add to thee. Let not mercy and truth forsake thee: bind them about thy neck; write them upon the table of thine heart: So shalt thou find favour and good understanding in the sight of God and man. Trust in the LORD with all thine heart; and lean not unto thine own understanding. In all thy ways acknowledge him, and he shall direct thy paths."

Isaiah 40: 8

"The grass withereth, the flower fadeth: but the word of our God shall stand forever." I believe in and find solace in the word of God, which I feel reigns true and supreme over all literature that has ever been written.

There is comfort in trusting in the Lord.

He Knows

Hebrews 4: 14-16

"Seeing then that we have a great high priest, that is passed into the heavens, Jesus the Son of God, let us hold fast our profession. For we have not an high priest which cannot be touched with the feeling of our infirmities; but was in all points tempted like as we are, yet without sin. Let us therefore come boldly unto the throne of grace, that we may obtain mercy, and find grace to help in time of need."

This is a very clear message.

First, we do not serve a God that cannot feel our pain, anguish, sorrow, hurts and all of the misfortunes that we go through. Even though He was tempted, just as we are sometimes, He sinned not. That's a great example for us to follow, even though we, or more specifically I, do not always pass the test.

Some days we can handle temptation better than others, but sometimes we want to strike back. Keep in mind, when we are having a not so good day, He knows. He will give us grace in time of need.

I have found that no matter what type of situation I find myself in, I should just stop and think for a minute and ask that His will be done, because His will is best for me. When I do that, I am moving myself out of the mix and putting Him first.

He said in Proverbs 3: 5-6, "Trust in the LORD with all thine heart; and lean not unto thine own understanding. In all thy ways acknowledge him, and he shall direct thy paths." In other words, we must come boldly to the throne and give all of our cares to the Lord, where we will find grace, mercy, and favor in our time of need.

Remember, Paul stated in 1 Corinthians 15:31, "I die daily," which we already learned in the previous section (Beatitudes versus Attitudes) means that every day something new is coming up. But, if we can just keep in mind that He knows all of our hurts and pain, we will be able to stay focused on the promises of God. There have been times in my life when I asked, Lord where are you? And then I had to remind myself, trials come to make me strong. Now, I am able to withstand my tests and trials because God said He would not put any more on me than I can bear.

Hebrews 4:14-16 tells us, "Seeing then that we have a great high priest, that is passed into the heavens, Jesus the Son of God, let us hold fast our profession. For we have not an high priest which cannot be touched with the feeling of our infirmities; but was in all points tempted like as we are, yet without sin. Let us therefore come boldly unto the throne of grace, that we may obtain mercy, and find grace to help in time of need." The profound revelation presented within these verses is that we have a High Priest that feels our infirmities and pain. He stands in the gap for us. He carries our burdens to the Father for us. He is well-aware of the problems we are faced with.

Our High Priest exercised His greatness by dying on the cross and rose for us while we were yet in our sin. He showed His love for us when we didn't even know how to love ourselves. When we allow the love of Christ to dwell on the inside of us, then it is a lot easier to love others.

Christ even loved the ones that hated and killed Him, that's awesome, that's also a lesson for us. It may be hard sometimes, but that is what He expects from us.

We are that light that sits on a hill and others are watching. It is not always easy, but He Knows. He will not allow us to go through anything that He has not gone through. When things seem to get us down we ought to repeat the words of the 23rd Psalm, which says: "The LORD is my shepherd; I shall not want. He maketh me to lie down in green pastures: he leadeth me beside the still waters. He restoreth my soul: he leadeth me in the paths of righteousness for his name's sake. Yea, though I walk through the valley of the shadow of death, I will fear no evil: for thou art with me; thy rod and thy staff they comfort me. Thou preparest a table before me in the presence of mine enemies: thou anointest my head with oil; my cup runneth over. Surely goodness and mercy shall follow me all the days of my life: and I will dwell in the house of the LORD forever.

So let us hold fast to our profession of faith in Him. The bottom line is, no matter what we might go through, God is there for us. We don't have to leave a message, we don't have to open up the computer, we don't need a cell phone number; He can hear all of us at the same time.

Now that's good news. We are all invited to the mercy seat where the love of our Savior, Jesus Christ abides.

Create and Renew

Psalm 51:10

"Create in me a clean heart, O God; and renew a right spirit within me." Here Nathan the prophet went in to talk to David after he had committed adultery with Bathsheba, who became pregnant and then David put her husband, Uriah, on the front line of battle and he was killed.

After David did this awful thing, he felt very sorrowful in his heart. Now the guilt set in. When the guilt of our lives sets in, it will bring us to our knees to ask for forgiveness.

Here David was making it personal. He used the word "me." He was not praying a generic pray, he was calling it just like it was.

That's what we need to do, confess our sins to God because Psalm 139 tells us, "O lord, thou hast searched me, and known me. Thou knowest my downsitting and mine uprising, thou understandest my thought afar off." Accordingly, God knows what we are going to do before we do it.

In Psalm 51: 10 David was doing what we need to do, ask God to create in us a clean heart and renew a right spirit within us. No matter what our sins may be, they will not dissipate until we ask God to purge us and make us whiter than snow.

According to Palms 25:7 David said, "Remember not

the sins of my youth, nor my transgressions: according to thy mercy remember thou me for thy goodness' sake, O LORD."

If we fail to give our sins to God, then we will end up empty and defeated. When we feel as though we have been broken, then we are where God wants us to be. Pride has been pushed aside, humility has set in.

David prayed for his inner renewal. He asked that God not take His spirit away from him. So we should be like David, and ask for a spiritual renewal.

We know when we are not right. All we have to do is repent of our wrongdoings and ask God to renew the right spirit within us, no matter what is going on around us or within us. As Paul was writing to the Romans in Romans 12: 1-2 he said, "I beseech you therefore, brethren, by the mercies of God, that ye present your bodies a living sacrifice, holy, acceptable unto God, which is your reasonable service. And be not conformed to this world: but be ye transformed by the renewing of your mind, that ye may prove what is that good, and acceptable, and perfect, will of God."

First, he said to present our bodies and then he said to prove it. We will be able to prove our lives when God dwells on the inside. God can create within us a new heart and renew the right spirit within us!

It's ours for the asking................

Psalm 46: 1-3

"God is our refuge and strength, a very present help in trouble. Therefore will not we fear, though the earth be removed, and though the mountains be carried into the midst of the sea; Though the waters thereof roar and be troubled, though the mountains shake with the swelling thereof. Selah."

We don't have to leave a voice message or send an e-mail. He is here right now. He said a present help. Right now!

When things are not going as we think they should, He is that present help, right now. God is an all knowing God. He knows what's going to happen even before we find ourselves in the middle of a travesty.

He is everything that we could ever want or need. When we think we are at the end of our rope, we just need a reminder of who is really at the end of the rope. It is Jesus Christ, Himself.

God tells us to "Be still, and know that I am God." (Psalm 46: 10)

Sometimes it is hard for us to be still, especially since we are still in the flesh. Nevertheless, He said be still. He will not leave us or forsake us. He is standing in the gap for us. Sometimes we don't know what to say or pray for, if we would just say Jesus, He will take our cares onto the Father.

When Moses was leading the people out of Egypt, God

gave Moses commandments to give to the people, "And Moses said unto God, Behold, when I come unto the children of Israel, and shall say unto them, The God of your fathers hath sent me unto you; and they shall say to me, What is his name? What shall I say unto them? And God said unto Moses, I AM THAT I AM: and he said, Thus shalt thou say unto the children of Israel, I AM hath sent me unto you." (Exodus 3:13-14)

So no matter what we go through, He said I AM, meaning I AM your bread, water, job, house, mother, father, problem solver, whatever, I AM.

When we have exalted all of our resources, I AM is a present help in time of trouble. That's a promise that we can stand on.

In this chaotic world we live in, it is truly a blessing to know He is here for us. We can have security when all else is insecure, just by knowing that He is a present help.

David said in Psalm 63:7, "Because thou hast been my help, therefore in the shadow of thy wings will I rejoice."

Psalm 145: 14

"The LORD upholdeth all that fall, and raiseth up all those that be bowed down."

I have been bowed down and God lifted me.

Jesus said in Matthew 11:28-30: "Come unto me, all ye that labour and are heavy laden, and I will give you rest." "Take my yoke upon you, and learn of me; for I am meek and lowly in heart: and ye shall find rest unto your souls." "For my yoke is easy, and my burden is light."

We can give God all of our troubles and He will see us through them all. He is a present help in time of need.

Pressing Toward the Mark

Philippians 3:13-14

"Brethren, I count not myself to have apprehended: but this one thing I do, forgetting those things which are behind, and reaching forth unto those things which are before, I press toward the mark for the prize of the high calling of God in Christ Jesus."

Here, Paul was referring to both his religious credentials, which now are counted as lost, as well as his Christian achievements and successes. In pursing his goals to know Christ, he is refusing to allow past errors in life to hold him back from reaching his goal of knowing Christ. He also refused to rest on past accomplishments.

A life of this sort could spell spiritual disaster, knowing that the "mark for the prize" is a life in God's Kingdom, which is too much to lose. There is no getting into the Kingdom, but through Christ Himself.

Knowing of Christ's suffering and dying on the cross for us, we should want to be more like Him, and not remain in our sinful selves. Paul told the people that he knew they were not all perfect, including himself, but they should continue, anyway, to press onward for a higher spiritual attainment, despite what was in their past. God is a forgiving God, no matter what our past has been.

None of us have "spiritually arrived," but we are pressing toward the mark of the prize. In looking back at our lives, we should be grateful about where we are today and where we could have been, or where we should have been, had it not been for the shedding of the blood.

"Finally, my brethren, rejoice in the Lord. Who shall change our vile body, that it may be fashioned like unto his glorious body, according to the working whereby he is able even to subdue all things unto himself." (Philippians 3: 1, 21)

I decided, I cried my last tear on yesterday, and now I am pressing toward the mark of the high calling.

What mark are you pressing for?

The Rocks Will Not Cry Out for Me

Luke 19: 28-31

"And when he had thus spoken, he went before, ascending up to Jerusalem. And it came to pass, when he was come nigh to Bethphage and Bethany, at the mount called the mount of Olives, he sent two of his disciples, Saying, Go ye into the village over against you; in the which at your entering ye shall find a colt tied, whereon yet never man sat: loose him, and bring him hither. And if any man ask you, Why do ye loose him? Thus shall ye say unto him, Because the Lord hath need of him."

Here Jesus entered into Jerusalem, He gave his disciples instructions on what to do and what to say in getting this colt that He was to ride on. When they entered into the village they found the very colt tied just as Jesus said it would be. After they brought the colt to Jesus they began taking off their outer garments and placing them on the colt. They began to praise and worship Jesus, which was a common expression. There were some Pharisees that did not agree with the praise and worship of Jesus.

The word tells us that He despises the contempt of the proud, but He accepts the praises of the humble. That's what the Disciples were doing.

With His entourage into Jerusalem, the Pharisees missed the King in human form. We should not allow others to miss the Christ that dwells on the inside of us by keeping Him all to ourselves.

Psalm 150: 1-6

"Praise ye the LORD. Praise God in his sanctuary: praise him in the firmament of his power. Praise him for his mighty acts: praise him according to his excellent greatness. Praise him with the sound of the trumpet: praise him with the psaltery and harp. Praise him with the timbrel and dance: praise him with stringed instruments and organs. Praise him upon the loud cymbals: praise him upon the high sounding cymbals. Let every thing that hath breath praise the LORD. Praise ye the LORD."

That's an awesome responsibility.

When the birds are chirping, they are praising Him. When the bees are humming that's their praise.

I am not ashamed to lift up His name, it does not matter where I am, for He said, "For whosoever shall be ashamed of me and of my words, of him shall the Son of man be ashamed, when he shall come in his own glory, and in his Father's, and of the holy angels." (Luke 9:26)

Amazing things happen when we lift up His name to others. Some might be lost and need directions back to Christ. Some might be discouraged and need some encouragement. It's simple; we cannot allow our silence to cause the rocks to cry out for us.

O Taste and See

Psalms 34

"I will bless the LORD at all times: his praise shall continually be in my mouth. My soul shall make her boast in the LORD: the humble shall hear thereof, and be glad. O magnify the LORD with me, and let us exalt his name together. I sought the LORD, and he heard me, and delivered me from all my fears. They looked unto him, and were lightened: and their faces were not ashamed. This poor man cried, and the LORD heard him, and saved him out of all his troubles. The angel of the LORD encampeth round about them that fear him, and delivereth them. O taste and see that the LORD is good: blessed is the man that trusteth in him. O fear the LORD, ye his saints: for there is no want to them that fear him. The young lions do lack, and suffer hunger: but they that seek the LORD shall not want any good thing. Come, ye children, hearken unto me: I will teach you the fear of the LORD. What man is he that desireth life, and loveth many days, that he may see good? Keep thy tongue from evil, and thy lips from speaking guile. Depart from evil, and do good; seek peace, and pursue it. The eyes of the LORD are upon the righteous, and his ears are open unto their cry. The face of the LORD is against them that do evil, to cut off the remembrance of them from the earth. The righteous cry, and the LORD heareth, and delivereth them out of all their troubles. The LORD is nigh unto them that are of a broken heart; and saveth such as be of a contrite spirit. Many are the afflictions of the righteous: but the LORD delivereth him out of them all. He keepeth all his bones: not one of them is broken. Evil shall slay the wicked: and they that hate the righteous shall be desolate. The LORD redeemeth the soul of his servants: and none of them that trust in him shall be desolate."

After reading this scripture for several years, I finally have decided to challenge myself to "Taste and see that the Lord is good." Yes, He is good. He has proven Himself time and time again. He not only hears our cries, He acts upon them. They that seek the Lord shall not want for anything.

I have come to realize that what God requires of me is to "Depart from evil, and do good; and dwell for evermore. For the LORD loveth judgment, and forsaketh not his saints; they are preserved for ever: but the seed of the wicked shall be cut off." (Psalm 37: 27-28) Because "The eyes of the LORD are upon the righteous, and his ears are open unto their cry." (Psalm 34: 15)

It seems that we are faced with evil each and every day of some sort, but the Lord will delivery us from it all. Sometimes God allows us to go into deep waters, not to drown us but to cleanse us. When we ask, "Lord where are you?" Know that He is still in the same place, sitting at the right hand of the Father interceding for us. In time He will bring us out all right.

Being Strengthened in the Midst of the Struggle

Matthew 8: 23-27

"And when he was entered into a ship, his disciples followed him. And, behold, there arose a great tempest in the sea, insomuch that the ship was covered with the waves: but he was asleep. And his disciples came to him, and awoke him, saying, Lord, save us: we perish. And he saith unto them, Why are ye fearful, O ye of little faith? Then he arose, and rebuked the winds and the sea; and there was a great calm. But the men marvelled, saying, What manner of man is this, that even the winds and the sea obey him!"

In this life, we all face challenges, difficulties, and times when things just don't go as planned. God does not send the storms, but He uses the struggles to help us grow and develop.

Every adversity is an opportunity for God's word to come alive in our lives, and see us to victory. God is still able to meet our needs in the middle of any struggles, then we will be able to see just how awesome He is really is.

Our struggles allow us to enlarge our vision and to see just how important it is to have God in our lives. In 1 Corinthians 15: 31 Paul said, "I die daily." Not physically, but he met with opposition every day, just as we do. Some days we have trouble on every side. No matter what bad thing(s) comes our way, Satan means it for bad, but God can take that same situation and bring good out of it, as discussed in Genesis 50.

So as we meditate on the promises of God, we can and will gain strength for whatever we are going through. If we allow Him to be the master builder of every area of our life, when we come against these struggles He will be there for us.

We must learn how and when to move ourselves out of the way. And let God....

The flesh introduces our mind to impurities, discord, jealousy, and so much more that is not of Christ. When we call on the name of Jesus to come to our rescue, He then puts those thoughts to rest with "the fruit of the spirit, which are love, joy, peace, patience, kindness, goodness, faithfulness, gentleness, and self-control", according to Galatians 5:22. When we are going through our struggles or storms, we just need to remember that God is there in the midst of it all with us and for us. And our labor has not been in vain.

When God said longsuffering, He did not put a time limit on it, He just said longsuffering. And sometimes I want to ask Him, "Lord isn't this long enough, where are you?" But I remember what David said in Psalms 23: 4, "Yea, though I walk through the valley of the shadow of death, I will fear no evil: for thou art with me; thy rod and thy staff they comfort me." That promise still holds true today.

So when we find ourselves in the midst of our struggles, we just need to be reminded that He is the strength for all of our struggles, no matter how large or small.

When we are going through our battles, we must remember, "We wrestle not against flesh and blood, but against principalities, against powers, against the rulers of the darkness of this world, against spiritual wickedness in high places." (Ephesians 6: 12)

The only way for us to win is to allow the Holy Spirit to dwell within our hearts. That is the only way we can and will win the battle and be strengthened in the midst of our struggles.

Becoming Complete

Philippians 1:3-6

"I thank my God upon every remembrance of you, Always in every prayer of mine for you all making request with joy, For your fellowship in the gospel from the first day until now; Being confident of this very thing, that he which hath begun a good work in you will perform it until the day of Jesus Christ:"

We all have dreams and visions for our lives. Sometimes we wait and wait and wait for them to come to pass. We pray and then we wait some more. We find ourselves standing on the promises of God, but sometimes it seems as though God has forgotten about us.

Becoming complete does not happen overnight. It actually starts the moment we accept Christ in our hearts. But our timeline is different from God's timeline. His ways are different from our ways. He is a God of completion. He will finish what He has started in our lives. He is also the author and finisher of our faith, as stated in Hebrews 12: 2. When we think He has forgotten, He is working behind the scenes on our behalf.

Sometimes we fall below His standards, but nevertheless we are becoming complete, we just have not arrived yet. The world sets the agenda for the professional man, but God is in control of the spiritual man.

We will not be complete until the coming of Christ Himself. So when we feel as though we have been left behind,

He is still there for us. He can still do His work through us. Therefore, let's not complain. Oftentimes, God allows us to go through things in order for us to have a testimony to help others to come to know who Jesus Christ really is.

I have many testimonies, things that have happened in my life and I know it was no one but God that brought me through. Even though he is not through with me, I will be complete one day, as long as I keep my faith and trust in Him.

Psalm 23

This meditation comes from the entire 23rd Psalm.

The words of David read as such:

Psalm 23

1. "The Lord is my shepherd; I shall not want.
2. He maketh me to lie down in green pastures; He leadeth me besides the still waters.
3. He restores my soul; He leadeth me in the paths of righteousness for His name's sake.
4. Yea, though I walk through the valley of the shadow of death, I will fear no evil: for thou art with me: thy rod and thy staff they comfort me.
5. Thou preparest a table before me in the presence of mine enemies: thou anointest my head with oil: my cup runneth over.
6. Surely goodness and mercy shall follow me all the days of my life; and I will dwell in the house of the Lord forever."

I grew up in Arkansas, my mother is a Sunday School Teacher and my father was a Deacon. It was important for us to learn this Psalm. It is powerful and strong. It gives us peace knowing that God leadeth us. My parents taught us this. Learning the 23rd Psalm was just part of the household routine.

Here David is reflecting on what God really meant to him. It is a personal relationship between Him and God.

When I read or recite the 23rd Psalm, I look at it as personal account of what and who God is to me.

Here David uses:

My---5 times

I------4 times

Me---7 times

Mine-1 time

That's very personal.

The Potter's Hand

Jeremiah 18: 1-6

"The word which came to Jeremiah from the LORD, saying, Arise, and go down to the potter's house, and there I will cause thee to hear my words. Then I went down to the potter's house, and, behold, he wrought a work on the wheels. And the vessel that he made of clay was marred in the hand of the potter: so he made it again another vessel, as seemed good to the potter to make it. Then the word of the LORD came to me, saying, O house of Israel, cannot I do with you as this potter, saith the LORD? Behold, as the clay is in the potter's hand, so are ye in mine hand, O house of Israel."

Jeremiah was commanded to go to the potter's house in order to learn a lesson. The potter's house was probably located in the southern section of the city or perhaps in the potter 's field south of Jerusalem, just beyond the valley of Hinnom.

The wheels were two circular stones connected by a vertical shaft. The potter could sit at the wheel, spinning the lower stone with his feet causing the upper disc to rotate. This enabled both hands to be free in order to work the clay. Should the vessel become marred or any impurity detected, the potter would not discard the clay, but simply remold it into another vessel.

No matter how broken we might think ours lives are, God is the potter and we are the clay. He can make, shape, and mold us into His likeness at any time He chooses. All we have to do is ask.

God taught the prophet Jeremiah what it meant to be a sovereign God. He taught him that God's plan would be fulfilled…one way or the other. Either his children would submit to gentle guidance or He would bring discipline to teach them the need for obedience. God has the last word over our lives.

So that leaves a question for us……Where do we stand?

We all fall short of God's perfectionness. We can ask to be put back on the potter's wheel if we truly want to be made perfect in His will. We are like clay in the hands of the potter. The Bible says in Romans 3:22-24, that we have all sinned and come short of the Glory of God. We can ask to be reshaped and molded so that we can be made perfect in His image.

If we do not repent and turn from our evil ways, just as God said to Jeremiah to tell the people that He would scatter them before their enemies, and I will show them my back and not my face in the day of their disaster or trouble. When we repent and ask for forgiveness we should turn from doing the things that please us and turn to pleasing God.

Jeremiah understood that God was the potter and He had control of the shape of the clay. How foolish it would be for the clay to complain or rebel. Since we are the clay in the potter's hand, which is God's hand, we do not need to complain, but ask to be made over in His likeness and not ours.

The potter will continue to mold the clay. But if the clay gets hard before it is complete, while it is in an unfinished state, he will crush it down and sprinkle it with water and begin again. God loves us so much that when we find ourselves doing wrong, He will sometimes allow us to be crushed so that He can raise us up again. The only way for us to become all that God desires us to be is to yield and remain moldable. We have no ability to shape ourselves.

The potter is creating something that is eternally beautiful. We are being conformed to the likeness of His Son. The potter's shaping is far better for us than anything we could ever imagine.

He is such a good and awesome God, so full of goodness, grace, blessings, forgiveness, and mercy we cannot even scratch the surface of His awesome holiness. Sometimes, when we think we've got it all together, that's when we need to give ourselves over to God. Because there are times, that we have a few rough edges that need to be removed. And sometimes He allows us to be crushed down so that His reshaping process can begin.

God is in complete control of our lives and all we have to do is ask Him to make us into the image of His Son and then we will be made whole. Let's remain moldable clay and yield our lives to the shaping of the potter's hand.

God sent His only Son Jesus, to earth for our sake, that we might have life and have it more abundantly, according to John 10:10. Jesus did not come to make God's love possible, but to make God's love visible. He gave His life for us. The least we can do is give our life back to Him. When we allow ourselves to be put back on the potter's wheel, then we can be that light that sits on a hill and others will see the workings of God in our lives.

In essence, we are like David when he said in Psalm 51: 7-12, "Purge me with hyssop, and I shall be clean: wash me, and I shall be whiter than snow. Make me to hear joy and gladness; that the bones which thou hast broken may rejoice. Hide thy face from my sins, and blot out all mine iniquities. Create in me a clean heart, O God and renew a right spirit within me. Cast me not away from thy presence and take not thy Holy Spirit from me. Restore unto me the joy of thy salvation and uphold me with thy free spirit."

Remember that nothing is small in the eyes of God. So do all that you do in love and He will be pleased. After all, He sees all that we do and He even knows the thoughts of our minds.

I want to be pleasing in His sight. One day, we all are going to stand before the throne of God and I want my good to outweigh the bad. I ask Him to shape me and mold me in His image and not mine. Because He is the potter and I am the clay!

Trusting God's Word

In trusting God's Word, I have come to the knowledge of what God has for me to do. That is to reach out and share my testimony with others. And always give Him the credit for doing what He has done in my life.

I always tell others that these are not my words, these are God's words. He was the one that told me what to do before I even knew that my husband would be leaving me. And I am so grateful that He saw enough favor in me and I am even more grateful that I was obedient.

Sometimes we have to go on blind faith, but if the Word or Voice is from The Lord, then we know we can trust it. After hearing His Word, I made some decisions that were not in my plans, but God knew what I would need before I was born. He knew the time and date my husband would die. He prepared me by telling me what to do. I am so glad I listened.

It is easy to sit back and hold on to ideas and think about the same thing for a long time. There is a difference when we put some action behind our thoughts and ideas.

I used to say, "Something or someone told me to do this or that." But now I do not say that anymore, I say God did. And then I put some action behind what I have been given to do.

Stand Still

When we stand still mentally, wait and listen for God's voice, He will lead and guide us in the right direction. Being still means taking time alone with God. We don't need to have someone around us at all times. That will allow us to get used to the empty nest that some of us find ourselves in.

I have found out that being still will allow me to silence the negative voices that sometimes run through my mind and my heart. At that time, I can choose the right thoughts and actions because then I will be able to measure them up with the Word of God. My thoughts should line up with His thoughts.

If we allow our hearts and minds to be still before Him, then and only then will He lead us into victory. We are still here and He has something for all of us to do.

The Lord shall fight for you, and ye shall hold your peace. A good Bible verse to read for this assurance is Exodus 14:14 KJV.

Whatever God has said in His Word is right and true. We can trust Him in all that He has said. So why do we put a question mark where God has put a period?

God has great plans for our lives, all we have to do is wait on Him and He will come through. He was in control then and is still in control now and forevermore.

It is Time to Make Some Changes and Move Forward

Now, it is time to make a change in our lives, and increase our faith and trust in God.

And He said to me, "My grace is sufficient for thee: for my strength is made perfect in weakness. Most gladly therefore will I rather glory in my infirmities, that the power of Christ may rest upon me." II Corinthians 12:9

Life is not easy for any of us. God did not tell us the road would be easy, but we have to persevere and keep God in the forefront of our lives. When we do it God's way we will make it to victory.

When We Say We Are Christians

When we say we are Christians, we are not really.

In 1 Corinthians 15: 31 Paul said, "I die daily."

We are striving to become Christians on a daily basis.

"Quote of the Day"

"I don't want to get to the end of my life and find that I have just lived the length of it. I want to have lived the width of it as well." – Diane Ackerman

Bio

Lydia Douglas, is a motivational speaker with a desire to help others realize that they have a well of untapped resources, unfulfilled dreams, and desires within themselves. She attended Forrest Park and Florissant Valley Community Colleges. She is a member of the National Speakers Club Organization and is a certified member of the Toastmasters Club. She has authored two other books, Stepping Stones to Success and Reaching Higher Heights.